WING

MATTHEW FRANCIS

Wing

FABER & FABER

First published in 2020
by Faber & Faber Ltd
Bloomsbury House
74–77 Great Russell Street
London WC1B 3DA

Typeset by Hamish Ironside
Printed in the UK by TJ International Ltd, Padstow, Cornwall

A CIP record for this book is available from the British Library

ISBN 978–0–571–35861–8

FSC
www.fsc.org
MIX
Paper from
responsible sources
FSC® C013056

10 9 8 7 6 5 4 3 2 1

Acknowledgements

Acknowledgement is due to the following, in which some of these poems first appeared: *Areté, Arty, Axon, The Best British Poetry 2014, Birdbook: Saltwater and Shore, The Caught Habits of Language, Epignosis Quarterly, The Guardian, The London Magazine, The Lonely Crowd, New Welsh Review, Poetry, The Poetry Review, Poetry Wales, Ver Poets Newsletter, Wild Court, Wired to the Dynamo.* The Micrographia poems featured in the exhibition 'The Secret Workings of Nature: Robert Hooke and Early Science' at the National Library of Wales in 2015, and I can be heard reading some of them on the National Library's You-Tube channel. 'Longhouse Autumn' is adapted from my article 'Ceredigion Autumn', first published in *PN Review*.

I have drawn on the following sources for facts and ideas: *The Observer's Book of Pond Life* by John Clegg, *Bugs Britannica* by Peter Marren and Richard Mabey, *Selected Poems of Dafydd ap Gwilym*, translated and edited by Rachel Bromwich, *Leech-doms, Wortcunning and Starcraft of Early England* by Oswald Cockayne, *Micrographia: or Some Physiological Descriptions of Minute Bodies Made by Magnifying Glasses* by Robert Hooke, *The Rose* by Jennifer Potter, *Food in England* by Dorothy Hartley, *The Herefordshire Pomona*, published on CD by the Marcher Apple Network, *Rain: Four Walks in English Weather* by Melissa Harrison, the website of the Mary Rose Museum, the website of the Royal Society for the Protection of Birds, information about Alsager Mere on the website of RM Cybernetics.

Thanks to Felicity Henderson for help on my Hooke project, to Katherine Levell, whose unpublished poem 'Camouflage' was an inspiration for some of the poems in the Canticles section, to Matthew Hollis, Lavinia Singer and all at Faber and Faber for all their help and support, to my friends at Aberystwyth University for feedback, and to Creina for everything.

Contents

FREEFALL

Longhouse Autumn 3
Mere 6
Waterbear 7
Frog, Crow 8
Sandwich Tern 10
Ladybird Summer 11
A Charm for Earwigs 12
Typewriter 14
Clock 15
Monomoon 17
A Dream of Cornwall 18
Freefall 20

MICROGRAPHIA

The Microscope 25
Ice, Snow 26
Sand, Gravel 28
Fishscale, Feather 30
Moss, Mould 32
Nettle, Bee-Sting 34
Wings of a Fly 35
Silverfish, Moth 36
Ant 38
Flea, Louse 40
Mealybug Nymphs, Gossamer 42
Creature 43

CANTICLES

Yellow 47

Wingscape 48

Rose Absolute 50

Elixirs 52

Liberty Caps 53

Wassail 55

Pomona 56

Devil among the Tailors 58

Collective 60

South and West 61

Sea Canticle 63

King of a Rainy Country 65

FREEFALL

Longhouse Autumn

An attic room stuffed with heat. I write at the window.
    Houseflies fizz out of the decaying frame,
        one every few seconds,
        as if they're breeding there.
Outside is a thicket of apple-trees, a japonica,
    roses the orange of a one-bar fire,
        a smear of sea beyond.

They built their houses long here. I live in half of one,
    a whitewashed slump of stone in the crook of a lane.
        When I stand outside
        on my forecourt of cobbles,
the village feels Mediterranean, dry as a gecko
    and crumbly as the unearthed fragments of some
        terracotta civilisation.

The hedge is stippled with blackberries, an anthracite harvest
    too rich even for the pigeons to finish.
        The semolina and jam
        of their droppings spatters the road
between strip fields spiked with rusty farm machinery.
    It leads to a church weatherproofed with slate
        and tending its flock of gravestones.

I walk on the low cliffs, doorsteps of sand and pebbles
    above the pick-and-mix shingle of the beach,
        my path strewn with flotsam:
        flotation-pods of seaweed,
crabshells, the fanned-out spindrift of plastic bottles,
    and, nesting in the bushes, a leathery
        mummified dogfish.

I share the evenings with someone else's furniture,
    balancing on the brink of an armchair
        to warm myself at the rose
        of my one-bar fire
that cowers in a baronial hearth, its chimney
    rising straight to the night sky. Peer up it
        and a star peers back.

I read, adrift in my double bed. Seaweed-green wallpaper
    lurks around the perimeter of the lamplight.
        When I switch off the day
        the dark comes up to my face,
and I hear its weight pressing on timbers and bedsprings.
    The village floats off through the night. I must swim
        to catch up with it.

∼

Through my office window, the sea grows bushes of shadow.
    Rivers of clarity crack the blue into plates.
        It looks for a moment as if
        you could walk on it.
There's a drowned country out there, the Parish of Underneath.
    If I gaze long enough it starts to loom back,
        blurry with eye-water.

A funny taste in the light, the copper tang of late afternoon.
    Sunset's a rose and lemon confection of clouds
        around the blood-yolk of sun
        breaking into the sea,
and the dark arrives in waves of iron-filing birds
    that swivel and balloon over the shoreline
        till the pier sucks them down.

[4]

We drive through the green convolutions of Wales, past a rock
    that's famous for its splurge of graffiti,
        Cofiwch Dryweryn – Remember
        a village gone under
the steel lid of a metropolitan reservoir.
    Evening keeps gaining on us, till the bus
        is a box of dirty light.

I step into a carboniferous night, the sweetness of coal-smoke,
    the amber of windows. I must go further
        through fields made spooky by
        the forms of grazing sheep
and a transit of pillowy wings, a barn owl.
In the mass of sea blustering behind my longhouse
        it's already winter.

Mere

for John Barnie

Today the mere turns a blind eye to the white overhead,
but when the wind gets up it shivers in its sequins.

There is blue in the bands around the stem of the dragonfly,
a few tatters of sunlight in the flowers of the yellow flag.

A heron mimes a pond ornament in the shallows,
as a mallard takes off from its runway of splashes.

The air above the bulrushes is granular with midges.
On the surface a pond-skater pilots a flotilla of dimples.

The metallic swivelling of roaches is no guide.
Following those arrows will get you nowhere.

There's a green finer than we can see, the hydra budding its
    offspring.
Another mere laps within the cell wall of the amoeba.

Waterbear

Pachyderm speck, comma of writhing
punctuating the volume of moss,
tardigrade, moss piglet, waterbear,

named for the heft of its eight-legged
trudging through the droplets that gum up
the broccoli forest it lives in.

The fumblings of its snub-limbed torso
are almost cuddly under the lens,
but it holds all its softness inside

with a crinkled skin tough as toenail
that can fend off the zeroes of space,
the scalding waters of sulphur springs,

and you can parch it for a decade,
till it's hard as a stranded loofah:
a drop of water and it pulses,

as if that was all there was to it,
back in the swim, setting off somewhere
in the lifeboat of its own body.

Frog, Crow

after Bashō

Into the old pond
a frog has just launched itself –
the water chirrups.

> A lone crow perches
> on a branch stripped of its leaves
> this autumn evening.

Frog-green, the pond's skin.
Its dark amphibian blood
swirls for a moment.

> Tree black as a crow,
> and the wind preening them both:
> feathered, featherless.

Most of those bubbles
belch from the pond's marsh-gas gut –
one swallowed hiccup.

> Deconstructed house,
> all open doors and windows,
> bare beams to sleep on.

Transparent life-forms
tumble in the tsunami,
flailing wisps of limb.

> Once, crows flew like leaves,
> a forest scratched at the sky
> with its upturned claws.

Cross-channel swimmer
in his wetsuit and goggles
breast-stroking the deep.

        Inky oak apples,
        a fungus hard as a shelf,
        and this excrescence.

Its first home was slime,
its siblings a soup of eyes.
Now it has legroom.

        Asleep, eyes open,
        on its misericord branch,
        it dreams it's a crow.

Slug-shiny water
where a small boy once caught frogs:
puddled reflections.

        Long after the splash
        has settled into darkness
        the crow tastes that green.

Sandwich Tern

It can't keep hold of its shaggy clump, shoulders the wind
and flaps upward before losing its purchase on the air
and circling back to where it came from, alighting,
a forgetful angel, with a benediction of wings.

But how should it know where to put itself, in this screechy
grassroots heaven among the blanched heads of thrift,
with the pixels of water blinking on and off all round,
in weather the grey and white of its plumage?

One touch of colour, the needle-nose pliers of its bill
dipped in yellow, a last trace of the yolk it was
before it hatched out into a cloudlet of chick
to be wrapped up in the cumulus of a wing.

Fed with the silver drool of sand eels that must have tasted
like everything it knew in that settlement of droppings,
it learned to embrace the air, to turn itself into a W
and plunge-dive into a shiver of bubbles.

In its summer bonnet of black, with a tuft sticking out behind,
that covers the eyes with a highwayman raffishness,
it stamped out its *dos-à-dos* with another dancer,
until a fish was plighted, and received.

Now it takes off and circles back, an absent-minded reader
whose eyes keep sliding to the end of the paragraph
and back again, re-reading its world, not knowing
which of its three elements it belongs to.

Ladybird Summer

That summer there was a plague of ladybirds, drifting
    over the garden in a reddish smoke.
        We'd find them on the carpet,
a smattering of coral beads from a broken necklace,
    but self-willed, crawling every which way, mating
        like tiddlywinks.

The flowering season for insects. Crickets twitched the grass,
    moths trundled under their paper-dart wings
        or crouched on the ceiling
in the circle of brighter light above the lampshade,
    and the mosquitoes balanced on the wall
        on moon-lander legs.

Trees split in the heat. We drove through a tawny country
    now turned to outback. In the pub courtyard
        we talked till the colour
drained from the petunias in the hanging baskets,
    unwilling to go home carrying the weight
        of the day's air.

There was too much summer. The ladybirds that gathered
    on ledges to be crunched by the closing windows
        had lost their picture-book brightness.
We were glad of the first sign of autumn, a bowl of plums,
    frost blooming on their skin, and tart sunshine
        in their yellow flesh.

A Charm for Earwigs

Witchy-beetle, forkin-robin,
no one heard you as you clambered
up the nursery slopes of pillow,

felt your way in heaving darkness
where a dreamer breathed siroccos,
scaled the north face of an earlobe,

stumbled on the antihelix
where the cartilage was ruckled
into an upended mizmaze,

teetered round its corrugations
to the vortex where the tragus
overhung a bloodwarm grotto.

There was curl-room in the concha
but the scent of earwax drew you
through a straight and oozy burrow

thrumming with a distant heartbeat.
First the walls were soft, then bony,
then antennae scratched a membrane.

Arrywiggle, horny-gollach,
you awoke me from my stupor,
rasping with a chitin stylus

on my mind's long-playing vinyl,
ratcheting my taut tympanum
with your cacophonic tarsi,

set my ossicles percussing
with the clangour of rough music,
dustbins, copper saucepans, kettles.

Now I smear a linen poultice
with the pulp of roasted apple,
press it, wincing, on my pinna.

Malic steam pervades my chambers
to entice you with a perfume
sweeter than November compost.

Clipshears, codgybell, twitch-ballock,
lift your bristles from my eardrum,
let the sea of cochlea settle,

turn back from the labyrinth.

Typewriter

One day you'll fetch the Smith Corona from the cupboard,
set it on the desk and unclasp its blue plastic shell
to expose the nakedness of its baby-grand workings.

Remember the punch and peck words had in those days,
the strain of Q in the little finger, the type head
leaning out on its stalk from its semicircular roost,

the angelus ting that marked the end of a line
the slap of the silver lever that jerked time forward,
the shift key that tilted the world on its fulcrum,

the grey formalities hedged by tabs and margins
that turned language into geometry, the braille
of the other side of the page under the fingertips?

What was struck here could never be unstruck,
in spite of backspacing and x's, packets of Tippex paper
and the vial of Snowpake, its screw-cap gritted shut.

Not used to taking ourselves so seriously, we prodded
at the ampersand tangled in its nest, the curly brackets
aiming their bows in opposite directions.

Switch on the anglepoise lamp; outside the window
it's carbon-paper dark. There's ribbonsmudge on your fingers
and a new sheet of foolscap rolled on to the platen.

Clock

The poet Dafydd ap Gwilym is disturbed in his sleep, c.1350

Once more he's walking through the streets of sleep
beside a grey wall with flowers growing out of it
running his right hand along its nubbly flank
    warm from the day's sun.

He's with a woman whose face he can never remember,
but she's wearing it now, because this is a dream.
She walks half-dancing, as a pony might.
    Her voice is a bell,

and the bell is a rider in armour crashing backwards
in an apocalypse of plates, flanges and rivets.
The lance is full in his chest. His helm rings
    and he wakes, gasping,

in the scratchy dark of a bed in some hostelry.
The bell has just stopped, but he can hear or see
the metallic squiggles of sound fading around him:
    the first clock in Wales,

so new it has no hands yet, only a bell
to cleave the night into hours. He pictures the weights
dragging the rope from its drum, cogs clacking out
    their brazen seconds.

Nearby, the monks are sleepwalking with candles
to pray in the sackcloth gloom of a chapel.
They've made a morning of their own, called Matins,
    for their dawn chorus.

The clock is a sleepless cobbler hammering
the blackness outside and inside his head,
a mill grinding it into particles
    that sift all round him.

But now he is feeling his way back to her,
by the crumbling wall held together by flowers
where they'll consort a little more, till the bell
    clangs it to bits.

Monomoon

O

rococo clock,
crown of fool's gold,
stook of corn,

clown's pompom,
ghost's cowl,
owl's down hood,

go soft
on woods, wolds
moors, rocks,

nod
to crops, cows,
shorn flocks,

throw off
spools of floss, whorls
of cottonwool blossom,

O

crock of frost,
brow of horn,
worn tooth.

A Dream of Cornwall

i.m. W. S. Graham

1

Now only the sea is ahead of us,
a meniscus of blue, unscratched by waves.
I feel we are driving into an eye.
Sometimes a glassy blip slithering across
makes me wonder if the eye is my own.

2

In the snug under the cliff
where leaves shaped like the ears
of lynxes, elephants, donkeys,
grow in a Max Ernst profusion,
we sweat in the hothouse steam
that reeks of wild garlic.

3

West of Zennor, foxgloves and red-hot pokers
incandesce in the rain. The land becomes pinched.
The fields are stone pens for a single cow.
A coach is winding round the lanes towards us.
We can see everywhere, as if we were flying.

4

I stand in the look-out hut
where men watched for the gleam
that meant the fish were returning,
and see the molten shoal
spit and leap on the surface.
There is no one to shout to.

5

A man is typing something in a cottage
by the pilchardy light of an oil lamp.
I am trying to read over his shoulder,
but the page is all consonants and obelisks,
and I am miles away in my childhood.

6

The sea is not yet dark,
a laundered cloth stretched over
the mahogany land,
as the candles of lighthouses
flutter their yellow. Tonight
we'll dine in the ocean.

Freefall

In memory of a friend killed in a parachute accident

1

Out of the metal shell of the plane, he hatched
into raucous air,

and stretched out, breathless, as he'd done so often,
on the cushion of wind,

to crawl, crablike, across the irregularities
of the buffeting element.

Tissues of cloud below swathed the greens and yellows
of a chequered world.

2

In the muffled glow of the flashgun I got for my twentieth
    birthday
he has the limp hair and high cheekbones of a glam rocker.

One evening the pavement became too pedestrian:
in mid-sentence he shinned up an iron lamp post.

Sinbad with saltwater tales of fabulous Scheherezades,
he tickled the froth on his pint with the tip of a finger,

while outside the weeping willows were washing their tresses
in the still waters of the St John's College punting pool.

3

When the parachute opens, you must feel for a moment as if
it's tugging you by the armpits,

kicking, away from the world, into the icy indigo
where air breathes its last.

And when it doesn't open, how strange that the fields below
should gather their softnesses

into a hurtling bludgeon, to smash one who reaches
towards them as home.

4

We climbed the stone tube of the stairs, our feet slipping on
     shine,
pausing sometimes to rest at an arrowslit of daylight,

and stooped though the last doorway into a space floored with
     planking.
and walled with the dazzle of vertigo. We looked over the side

at the dorsal feathers of flying pigeons, disconcerting
as the back of one's head seen in the hairdresser's mirrors,

at the pinhead figures trailing their elongated shadows,
and at the end of our lives, ten seconds away from here.

5

Step through the hatchway of sleep. The lurch you feel
will subside in a heartbeat.

You voyaged every night to these upper regions,
falling from the earth

with downy seeds, with the spiderlings that drift here,
so much higher for them.

Sleep on the wing, the way swallows are said to,
sleep on the wing.

MICROGRAPHIA

after the scientific treatise by Robert Hooke (1665)

The Microscope

This morning the sun nuzzles the glass.
    Outside, the lawn and squared stone
    of the College are set out,
        irrefutable,

but I am working in panelled gloom
    and the smell of musty books.
    I have trapped some of the day
        in a square mirror

so that it lights up a specimen
    fixed to a movable plate
    at the end of a brass tube.
        I peer through the dark,

at an object that used to be small,
    now held in this cylinder
    that feels like part of my eye,
        a round, silent place.

There is nothing in it but myself
    and this morsel of nature,
    its chambers and projections,
        armour plate, pincers,

more complex than I had suspected.
    Only the flaws in the lens
    prevent my seeing deeper.
    I study and draw.

Ice, Snow

Overnight, a soft frost
    on angle and cornice,
        brick, bark, stone, whatever

the cold air could get at,
    not the hoar frost bristling
        with splinters of razor,

but a fluff cumulus
    like the beard on old jam.
        It sharpens, through the lens,

to six-sided clearness,
    hollow rods already
        nibbled by the sun's warmth.

~

This foul-water vessel
    is frozen to topaz,
        the surface feathery

with scrollings of icework
    as on a chilled window.
        Ice ferns grow from one root,

the main stems raised, whiter
    than the offshoots which run
        straight or curling from them,

and the offshoots' offshoots,
    flowerless and seedless,
        not tasting of urine.

~

A black hat left outside
    in falling snow becomes
        barnacled with white stars,

each of a new species.
    Six arms, spiny, plated,
        scalloped, or decked with orbs,

seeming identical,
    but the lens shows ice-galls
        from thawings and freezings,

their cloud-grown symmetries
    broken on the way down
        in the fray of armed flakes.

Sand, Gravel

The parcel proved to be full of sand,
as if my friend had sent me a present of an hour
with no glass to keep it in.

I fingered the soft dune on my desk.
It was not dried estuary sludge or the crumblings
of Alum Bay's sunset cliffs,

but the East Indies milled to powder.
Magnified, there were sapphires, emeralds and rubies,
pieces like blocks of crystal,

tumbled about as in a quarry,
some shapeless, others geometrical. I saw prisms,
cones, pyramids, ovals, spheres,

one spiral of white I kept losing
when I turned from the lens. I had it again, swept it
off to the side with a pin.

It was the size of a grain of flour
but I counted twelve twists on the coiled chalk of the shell:
some tiny mollusc lived here,

a residence hewn from a dustmote.
The least part of the world is greater than we had guessed,
so that the world as a whole . . .

I thought as I used my chamber pot.
When I had oozed the last of my wet fire, a spoonful
of gravel lay in the base.

This, too, I examined, marvelling
at its layers of mica, at the glinting edges
of rhomboids and rectangles.

Fishscale, Feather

Fish out of water,
or rather the canvassy
hide of one, brown-speckled as a map.
When I stroke it the wrong way
it rasps my finger –

I've raised the hackles
of its overlapping scales.
Calmed, they are fingernail-smooth, only
a shifting pattern of sheen
hinting at ocean.

When I tweeze one out,
I can see the oblong tab
that lodged in the skin, the fluted end
that poked through on the inside,
holding it in place,

while the outward fish
merged into the sea-floor, cased
in scallop-shell scabs of muddy horn,
each carved with ridges and grooves
and a fringe of spikes.

This link of chainmail
forged for an undersea life
is adrift through the dry of my room,
as this feather has settled
with no wing to lift.

It is mostly air.
Even the quill, sliced open,
is crammed with a white pith of bubbles,
and air snags in its million
butterfly-kiss threads.

I part them, observe
the fibres that lock the mesh.
A wipe of the bird's bill could close them,
as I do with my fingers,
mending the torn silk.

Nothing is so light
and strong as this blade of down
plucked out of the air. Now I record
its woven mathematics
with another one.

Moss, Mould

I magnify the green of walls, the cushion of fur
that darkens the lawn and softens the garden seat.
Bushy sprouts rise from a hairy parsnip root,
tipped with hard cases I cut with my knife

to find it crammed with cottony stuff.
A second case inside that
is full of a white powder.

Does moss grow from such dust
or spring of itself

from damp and rot?

~

Bricks, wood, bones, leather, even stones decay. Moss lodges
in their nooks and soft places. I shall say nothing
of how I've seen it furnish a dead man's skull,
the rough bone now as welcoming as bark.

Things forget what they were, and become
what they are made of. Rain, air, mulch,
nourish this first and last green,

now open like a watch
for me to peer at

live wheels and springs.

~

A sodden forest of books: you can smell it growing.
The mould is blooming on this one, shaggy smudges
of white growth fingering the sheepskin cover.
The animal that it once was is sick.

Enlarged, the white is mushrooms, fine stalks
bent by the weight of their round heads,
some young and smooth, some ageing,

the heads torn to flitters
as the plants ripen

their crop of stink.

~

Summer. The roses get on with their perfumed business,
but I am looking at the leaves, dry in the heat
and mottled with yellow stains, the undersides
scabbed with hillocks of a gummous substance.

From these amber beds stalks are growing
each with a black pod on the end
as for invisible seeds.

If so, they are so small
ten thousand would not

make this full stop.

Nettle, Bee-Sting

You have been ambushed among the hedgerow's foliage
by such a leaf. You know its dragon-tooth outline,
the frizz of pale hairs that had it in for you.
But now look at it. Each hair is a spike
fit to impale a traitor's head on,
hollow, clear as an icicle.
I brush it with my finger.
I see the molten-glass
sap rise in it, feel
its wisp of fire.

And this harpoon
with its cat-claw hooks,
its tip that protrudes from
a sheath with hooks of its own
to pierce, grapple, inject and pump,
self-willed engine of gripe and spasm
that tears the innards out of the wielder,
is the whole point of a bee, the argument
a posteriori, what those hummed undertones
in summer lanes were getting at, the price of honey.

Wings of a Fly

I have watched small flies
strumming the air above the river,
and tried to see the blurred edge of the wingbeat
that kept them (more or less) where they were,

and a bluebottle
playing blind man's buff with the window
or reeling across my room, a crooked flight
as of one who would fall if he could.

Glued to a feather
and prodded with a nib, he took off
in a faint aura of wings, so I could guess
at the form and motion inside it,

the down-and-forward
plunge of it, the up-and-backward lift,
then the tilt down and down-and-forward again.
The sound was like a bowed viol string.

I have heard that song
many long afternoons, high or low
according to the instrument that made it,
fretting at the tautness of my mind.

When I had stilled it,
I studied the leaves of wing, curled veins
with a glassy membrane between them, pleated
and stuck all over with fine bristles.

Silverfish, Moth

One swish of itself and it vanished
into the alley between two books.
There was a twilight city in there,
    leather and paper and dust,
where it had eaten itself a home.

You see it mostly going away,
a virtuoso of departure,
all tail, flickering into absence.
    Its shine is a non-colour,
the blankness of cloud in a window.

At last I had one, the tapering
torso of linked, metallic segments,
the helmet of head with four feelers,
    three more feelers on the tail –
feeling, like fleeing, is its business.

They call it bookworm. Its soil is words.
It is a fish that swims in the dry,
a full-grown caterpillar, a moth
    that flits among the pages,
having no need of wings. Unlike this

plumed moth, its four wings soft as an owl's,
a tired angel I found on my wall
in the splayed pose of proclamation.
    It was tufted all over,
body, legs, wing-stalks, even the horns,

brushes of fibres to catch the air.
The plumage differed, like that of birds,
according to the part it grew on.
        Days later I was finding
white bits lodged in my skin, moth-feathers.

Ant

All afternoon a red-brown trickle
    out of the roots of the beech
       and across the lawn,
a sort of rust that shines and dances.
    Close up, it proves to be ants,
       each droplet a horned
traveller finicking its way round
    the crooked geometry
       of a grass forest.
A finger felled in their path rocks them
    amazed, back on their haunches.
       I see them tasting
the air for subtle intelligence,
    till one ventures to scale it,
       and others follow.

They are fidgety subjects to draw.
    If you sink the feet in glue
       the rest twists and writhes;
kill one, the juices evaporate
    in seconds, leaving only
       the shrivelled casing.
I dunked one in brandy. It struggled
    till the air rose from its mouth
       in pinprick bubbles.
I let it soak an hour, then dried it,
    observed the spherical head,
       the hairlike feelers,
the grinning vice of its sideways jaw,
    the metallic carapace
       with its scattered spines.

Some draught stirred it then. It rose to all
    its feet, and set off across
        the rough miles of desk.

Flea, Louse

These intimates are
assiduous as servants
    and close as lovers.
They have always been with us.
    Niggling reminders,
marginal notes in fine print,
they are what we come down to,
    an itch.

This armoured teardrop
bestuck with shining bodkins,
    its seven-league legs
hitched up ready for leaping,
    knows us with feelers
and probing snout. We wear it
next to our skin, our blood-nursed
    offspring.

And this cone-headed
clamberer, its abdomen
    garnished with bobbles,
one of its six hooks clutching
    a hawser of hair,
has grappled with all of us.
We are its wildwood, its prey
    and home.

I starved it some days
then suckled it on my finger,
        watched as the red pumped
into blood-blister chambers,
        an inward heartbeat,
the tarry droppings it left
soiling my skin with my own
                used blood.

        When you read my book,
unfold these ingenious
        pages of monster,
pore over the ABC
        of schemes and figures,
and learn how much small there is.
Think of its pincers and probes,
                and scratch.

Mealybug Nymphs, Gossamer

A warm wall, heavy leaves, hard green grapes
    and a cluster of berries
        spun out of cobweb.

They were packed with brown roe, or, later,
    an anarchy of hatchlings,
        scattering crawlers

scarce larger than the eggs they once were,
    two eye-dots on a body
        the shape of an egg.

I counted nine scales at the rear end,
    two whiskers, a two-pronged tail,
        six legs underneath.

Though I shut some in a box, thinking
    they might become something else,
        they grew but little,

leaving me with these wisps of knowledge,
    like the filaments that fall
        sometimes from the air,

which may be the shed tissue of clouds
    or thrums of unfinished web.
        I cannot join them.

Creature

Reading one September day
I felt it tickle the page
as if one of the letters
had broken free of the words.

It held two claws out in front,
the way a blindfolded man
protects himself from the wall.

I do not know what it was,
but I have set it down here

in case you should meet with one.

CANTICLES

Yellow

You crack the shell and think there is yellow in everything.
It has claimed a sector of tablecloth, warms your right hand
as you go prospecting with a teaspoon for liquid yellow,
and scrape a lump of fridge-hard butter across your bread.
A few Easter cards stand on the sill with their yolk-coloured
    hatchlings,
beside a vase of daffodils blaring through their megaphones.

Not long after the first crocuses fingered through the earth,
the lawn is raging with dandelions. Look at the primroses,
each with a darker star at the centre of its corona,
and the forsythia spraying lemon by the fence.
What are they warning us about with their high-vis signage?

The lane is blazoned with heraldic suns of celandines,
and beacons of gorse and broom catch across the hills.
It's there in the ring round the eye of a blackbird.
The first brimstone of the year, a floater at the edge of your
    vision,
dithers like a sunflake cast by a stained-glass window.
A bronze thrumming in the cowslips reminds you of honey.

You crack the world and yellow runs out with the green.

Next come the buttercup meadows with their millions in gold,
and then one evening in May you'll drive down the coast
with the overgrown hedgerows of laburnum on one side of you,
Welsh sheep fields hung with accessories by Klimt,
and a blob of yellow on the other, softening into the sea.

Wingscape

The path grinds itself into the feet. A grayling skitters
from under the boot toe, and settles a stone's kick ahead.

A few wings of summer left: a chalkhill blue,
like a stemless harebell, flailing around the ankles,

a holly blue dulled to lavender, a small blue dusted with brown,
a silver-studded blue vanishing into the sky.

Sun zings off the scrapheap. A cranesbill has taken root,
and a grizzled skipper buzzes at it to salvage the usable.

The slow handkerchief of a large white waves in the railway
   siding
where the rosebay willowherb is spinning its floss.

The days won't keep still. At the entrance to the field,
where brambles smother the stile, a gatekeeper hovers.

A comma is suspended in the woodland margin.
A white-letter hairstreak is one scribble among many.

In the clearing the Duke of Burgundy flies its orange blazon.
The Queen of Spain fritillary is dancing in the shadows,

while the purple emperor parades under the canopy
before alighting on a collation of pony dung.

And, where the buddleia toasts itself by the garden fence,
a peacock comes, wearing its plumage of eyes,

and a red admiral shuffles on a finger of purple,
each antenna tipped with a pinhead of gleam.

Rose Absolute

Bristling Junos with crinoline heads, the hybrid teas
with their crimp and whorl are airy as marshmallows,
the sunsets of suburban gardens, Fragrant Cloud, Crimson
    Glory,
and Peace the colour of a late sky, custard curdled with rhubarb.

After dark in the rose garden, floribunda and grandiflora
are sculptures of marble and shadow, laced with barbed wire.
We've shut the gate on the dogrose, blood relative of the bramble,
confettiing the summer hedgerows, on the baked-apple
    sharpness of eglantine,
and the musk rose that scent-marks the spinneys in September.

Long ago snagged by the *alba*, a Maiden's Blush crumpled in
    tissue,
its whitesoft tangle of lingerie, its sudsy innocence,
we were physicked by *Rosa gallica*, the Apothecary's Rose,
roundels of strengthening burgundy nursing yellow wisps at
    the heart,
wandlets of philosophical gold. We sweetened our breath with
    the pills
that Nostradamus concocted from four hundred powdered
    roses,
with sugar of roses, syrup of dry roses, honey of roses.

Red roses are under Jupiter. They clear sight, soothe a rasped
    throat,
the griefs of bladder, gum, fundament; St Anthony's fire.
Simmer them with spikenard, balsam, aloes, the gall of a crow,
the urine of a virgin youth. Seethe them with camomile,
    lavender

and twenty swallows pounded to pulp in a mortar.
This is oil of swallows. Your aches will wheel off on long wings.

The *centifolia* is a Roman orgy of fondling petals,
and the moss rose has a muffler of greenery round its throat.

In Bulgaria the pickers are holding hot buds between their
    fingertips,
smoking the Turkish-delight roll-ups they've candied
with balls of rose-gunk scraped from their thorn-hardened skin.
Soon they'll move off through hectares of damask rose east
clouded with steam from copper stills and steel-piston factories
where they brew the attar of roses and the rose absolute, rusty
    oils
that cling to boudoir and petticoat with their musk and
    ambergris.

I found a rose on the pavement once, colourless in the
    streetlight
and took it back to look at under the anglepoise,
observing the high-necked elegance of its Chinese ancestors
that the plant-hunters found flashing their silks in mandarin
    gardens,
Fortune's Double Yellow, Hume's Blush Tea-Scented China,
    Parson's Pink China.
This one had Slater's Crimson China in its bloodline.
Some lovers must have dropped it. It had the complicated
    stillness
of a petalled merry-go-round that has just stopped turning.

Elixirs

after the Old English Lacnunga

These have potency against nine venoms
and against nine flying things,
against odious matter dispersing over the land:

sludging of Milk of Magnesia from a poison-blue bottle,
uprush of Alka-Seltzer, headlong towards clarity,
Disprin, a clouded moon fuzzing at the bottom of the cup,

against worm blast, against water blast,
mineral sift of Beecham's Powders, a formula unfolded,
gulped sunset of Haliborange that sinks into fishiness,

against thorn blast, against thistle blast,
luminous inchworm of Germolene squeezed from the tube,
water-green TCP, fragrance of gnat-haunted evenings by the
    river,

against ice blast, against venom blast,
cough mixture, honey and lemon, garlicky linctus of Liqufruta,
tidal-wave whisper in the ear canal, warm olive oil.

Liberty Caps

When we rose in the morning the sky was the grey-pink of
    mushrooms
and we moved through the asphalt gills of the town, feeling our
    way
to where the fields were. The grass was longer than we expected.
We remembered caravan summers, white presences in the dew.
They are never there till they are, insidious and sudden as
    daylight,
the parrot wax cap of dawn unfolding its red and orange.

We were looking for the magic psilocybin, the liberty cap,
shaky-stemmed thimbles of hallucinogenic tomfoolery,
but found only an unidentified breakfast, marquees of field
    mushrooms,
aniseed bruisers of horse mushrooms, a Renoir dalliance of
    parasols,
the giant puffball resting its meringue bulk on the field,
a fairy ring of darkened grass as if a cloud was passing inside
    the earth,
where the fungi stretched out their webbing, while buff pimples
    broke out on the surface.

We'd seen poisoners in pictures, the yellow stainer bleeding
    chrome ink,
the panther, the pallid droop of the destroying angel's plumage,
deathcaps the queasy green of a hospital wall. Would we know
    them in the flesh?

Only the fly agaric, a madcap in red-and-white motley,
but it was autumn in the woods when we found those, and we
    knew better,

avoiding the russulas with their paintbox colours, green,
    golden and purple,
the Noddy-red caps of the shining russula and the sickener,
and the trooping crumble-caps making their way down
    a rotten log.

We were looking for the charred trumpet of the horn of plenty,
the golden trumpet of the chanterelle with its scent of apricots,
the glazed crust of a penny bun shining among leaf crumbs.
In the smell of damp woodwork, the trees braced themselves
on the hardness of brackets and polypores, the beefsteak
    fungus, red
as a Sunday joint in a doll's house, yellow chicken of the woods.
We winced from the ooze of black witch's butter, from jelly
    antlers
from the shaggy earth tongue and the fly-draped phallus of a
    stinkhorn,
but found mauve wood blewits, the amethyst deceiver,
a rubbery hedgehog with its needles underneath, a brain fungus
crinkled and resinous between the roots of a pine.

Earthstars were coming out underfoot, the rosy earthstar
peeling and offering itself, inedible fruit on a basket of parings,
the collared earthstar on its crumbly, clay-coloured ziggurat,
the arched earthstar, an H. G. Wells Martian on four straining
    stilts,
as we made our way back with baskets of slug-fretted fungi,
while the liberty caps rioted on the verge by the police station.

Wassail

Shut the door against the dark, the chilblain prickle of stars.
Heat a poker in the coals till it's red as a sore finger,
plunge it in the tankard till the ale snorts and gargles,

summon the spirits of bumpo and hot buttered rum,
brown Betty with toast in her hair, and an aura of nutmeg and
    ginger,
the blue blazer, an ectoplasm of flaming brandy,

the jubilance of a cardinal crimson with claret,
a bishop bearing the orb of a clove-spiked orange,
a pope golden and ebullient with champagne,

rumfustian and eggnog, thick custards softer than bedclothes,
caudle and ale berry, starchy as a well-warmed nightshirt,
spinster's blush with the heat of port surging through it;

stand on the kitchen table to froth the ale from a height,
juggle the Scottish hot pint from one jug to the other,
stir with a twig of sweet briar, a wand of cinnamon.

Wassail will be our weather, a heat haze of grog and toddy.
We'll fill the night with the scent of ypocras, the glow
of the puckered moons of roast apples in a bowl of lambswool.

Pomona

'There's a dish of Leathercoats for you.'
    The Herefordshire Pomona

Pink of a warm evening, the Joanneting looms over the soft
    fruit.
It's too soon for the Early Spice, but here is the Early Harvest
with a faint blush on the side next the sun, the Laxton's Early
    Crimson,
the Early Julien strewn all over with dots and whitish specks.
The bare flesh of a Summer Strawberry reddens after the bite,
while a flabby gourd of Sack and Sugar rots on the tree,
and an Irish Peach is fuzzy with wasps on the lawn.

Maggots are delving in the glassfibre of the Transparent Codlin
as autumn spatters the lanes with Redstreaks and Red Splashes.
The Carrion Apple moulders. Foxwhelps scurry underfoot.
The steam of baked Norfolk Beefings sweetens a fat sunset,
as we pay our respects to the Queen of Sauce, the Beauty of
    Kent,
and inside its pastry sarcophagus the Catshead is sultry as
    Egypt.

A hothouse smell of Pitmaston Pine Apples in the cellar.
Lightbulbs in the dimness, a basket of Golden Pippins,
a coffer of Golden Nobles, loose nuggets of Golden Knobs,
the sweetshop munificence of Coe's Golden Drops
and the elongated shadow of a Golden Spire.

Here are the russets in their leather coats, the Aromatic Russet,
the Boston Russet with its pilgrim wholesomeness,
the Caraway Russet with the seedcake fragrance of aunts.

[56]

We have brought our offerings to the King of the Pippins
and found only the glower of a Striped Monstrous Reinette.

The air has a bite to it now, White Must, a Hoary Morning.
A Winter Coleman holds out grey arms in the orchard.
A Pigeon plumps itself in the cold, and mistletoe makes its
    nests
on the rough battlements of the Tower of Glamis.

When the last Gloria Mundi has fallen, where is our Seek No
    Further?
The ancient Ribston Pippin tree slumps on its crutches
while the Ribston Pippins sleep out the winter in newspaper,
old Ribston Pippins mulling their spices and parsnippy sugars.

Devil among the Tailors

The fuse of autumn is smoking. There is nothing for it
but to make a man out of oddments and slump him against
    a gatepost,
his face a flame-yellow rictus sooted with shadows.

Then maybe the glass case in the sweetshop will be gaudy again
with tubes, drums and cones, their coloured wrappings topped
with a flourish of blue touch paper like the twist of salt in the
    crisp packet:

the Chrysanthemum Fountain planted under the glass,
its brassy petals in-folded, beside a Flower Pot
where the shoots are still not stirring in the black powder,

the dormant volcanoes, Mount Etna and Mount Vesuvius,
Aeroplane and Whirlibird squatting on stubby wings,
mute Screech Owl and Banshee, the Humming Spider holding
    its breath,

Skybolt and Sun Burst, Pole Star and Cape Canaveral,
rockets not yet fitted with sticks, with that amputated look
of the head of a lorry with no trailer attached.

There will be time to hoard them in shoeboxes, study the small
    print:
Emits a star cluster with screecher, screamer and air bomb;
shake the Mine of Serpents so the snake eggs rattle inside it,

assemble an arsenal of Atom Bombs, Block Busters, Aerial
    Torpedoes,
the Jumping Jack's drab zigzag of industrial tubing
and a contraption of clustered cylinders called Devil among
    the Tailors.

Because the season won't burn itself, or only very slowly,
with the brown crinkling of a jacket potato,
we must scrabble up its leavings into a bonfire,

and find a penny for the guy, or your thoughts.
These new dark nights need something to set them off:
a Golden Zodiac, Butterfly Twinkler, Feathery Fire.

We'll meet at arms' length, lighting one sparkler from another
in a metal kiss till the magma bead at the centre brightens,
showering the garden with sparrowclaws of light.

Collective

Down the gallery of long grasses torchlit by foxgloves,
our tread haunted by the gibber
of a poltergeist of larks.

Cursive tracings
in invisible ink:
a calligraphy of swallows.

Slackropes of wire festoon the village,
teetered upon
by a funambulism of jackdaws.

Recapitulating
on the last outposts of daylight,
a double-take of blackbirds.

Their klaxoning sounding the outbreak of winter,
their insignia on the blank sky:
a chevron of geese.

In the town square a puppetry of pigeons;
around the back-alley dustbins
a pillage of seagulls.

Winterflush over the pier
paisleyed
with a shifting mandelbrot of starlings.

South and West

Outside Child's Ercall cat's paws of sleet speckled the wind-
   screen.
Preston Gubbals was not much more than a dovecote without
   its doves,
but there was a rough warmth in the hewn sandstone of
   Ruyton-XI-Towns.
Crossing the ford at Neen Savage, the tyres sprouted wings
   of water.
Hopton Cangeford was morris dancing in its tassels of
   daffodils.
From Angelbank we looked down on squares of silver and
   fool's gold.

We spent the night in a layby near Hope under Dinmore,
beneath the Brutalist shadows of parked juggernauts.

Not yet lunchtime at Trumpet. The malty alcoves of the pub
   were deserted.
At Upper Framilode the Severn gazed out through eyelash reeds.
At Engine Common the fields had slumped into green
   wrinkles.
Sun pinkened the church at Acton Turville, brought Vobster
   out in a rash of daisies,
ruffled the stone heads on the gateposts at Mappowder.
We smelt the dank of wild garlic at Ryme Intrinseca,
and gargoyles spat from the church tower of Toller Porcorum.
Whitchurch Canonicorum cowered under rainclouds of thatch.
Oath was shivery in the twilight, and Catcott Burtle
gathered the smoke of coal fires round it by way of a blanket.

Monksilver was a catastrophe of morning bells
as if we'd broken it. The Bronze Age yew at Ashbrittle
was a senile labyrinth, all gnarls and needled glooms.

The moor slouched on the horizon. The grass
was strawed with last year's yellow when we reached
    Sticklepath
and stretched our legs on its lichen-splotched slab of bridge.
At Queen Dart tussocky ponies browsed among the primroses,
and we passed Upton Hellions and Pancrasweek
in a loosening of the air, an erosion of all those accretions
of cottages, hedges, and churches, of names and stones.
Before us was simple blue, and Washaway, Stoptide, Pityme.

Sea Canticle

The ship settles on the bottom to lie on her side,
as the flatfish do.

Plaice and dragonet shuffle away, megrim and witch
shake the silt from their skirts.

Porbeagle, smoothhound and tope nose round the hull.
Sea-needles probe her.

Blonde ray and thornback ray flap white undersides at her,
smiling through ghostly sheets.

Day is a cloudy green. Night blinks with the phosphorescence
of sea-pens and comb jellies.

There is a crust to grow: limpets and barnacles, jellied stalks
of dead men's fingers.

Brown and white plumose anemones take root in the rigging.
Sea-oranges cluster on deck.

Brittle star, sun star and velvet crab graze over a carpet
of breadcrumb sponges.

Here is a pewter tankard, a sundial in its leather case,
a shoal of gold coins,

the surgery with its stoppered bottles and metal syringes,
a bowl for bloodletting,

the galley with square trenchers and two brass cauldrons,
spoons of silver and wood,

the bones of five men and a powder monkey beside their
    culverin,
bundles of arrows.

Centuries of summers blow over, blue breezes of mackerel
that veer and flick on,

before the trawl net snags, before the first diver, blurting
    bubbles,
flounders over her.

King of a Rainy Country

Je suis comme le roi d'un pays pluvieux.
BAUDELAIRE

A fine day for the coronation. Waterdogs process across a blue carpet of sky bearing the regalia of sunshine.

He is haloed in Scotch mist, waving from a tissuey cape of smirr. We blink away smither.

An unseasonal squall, the organ voluntary drowned out by the blunk of a cow-quaker.

He wakes to a blashy morning. The palace gutters dunk outside the window, beggar's barm swirls in the courtyard.

He rides out in the dinge to inspect his fens: the Forty-Foot Drain, the dykes and sluices at Queen Adelaide, the pumping engine at Prickwillow.

What kind of progress is possible through these stoachy acres? One clashy stile after another, the land all of a pop.

He is guest of honour at a fox's wedding, launches a ship to the spitter of applause, snips a soggy ribbon in the dibble.

He rides back over the tops, looking back at the grey of a moor-gallop in cold pursuit.

He shivers on a snivey day. He'd settle for snow, the Ross Ice Shelf or the South Sandwich Islands. Perhaps this gosling blast is a harbinger.

Some empire, this soss, stott, plother. You can't see the borders. It doesn't look as if it will ever stop.